To

From

Date

KID DEVOS

ABOUT SELF-CONTROL

Kid

50 Devos

DEVOS

Scripture quotations are taken from:

The Holy Bible, New International Version (NIV) Copyright © 1973, 1978, 1984, by International Bible Society. Used by permission of Zondervan Publishing House. All rights reserved.

The Holy Bible, New King James Version (NKJV) Copyright © 1982 by Thomas Nelson, Inc. Used by permission.

Holy Bible, New Living Translation, (NLT) copyright © 1996. Used by permission of Tyndale House Publishers, Inc., Wheaton, Illinois 60189. All rights reserved.

The Message (MSG)- This edition issued by contractual arrangement with NavPress, a division of The Navigators, U.S.A. Originally published by NavPress in English as THE MESSAGE: The Bible in Contemporary Language copyright 2002-2003 by Eugene Peterson. All rights reserved.

New Century Version®. (NCV) Copyright © 1987, 1988, 1991 by Word Publishing, a division of Thomas Nelson, Inc. All rights reserved. Used by permission.

International Children's Bible®, New Century Version®. (ICB) Copyright © 1986, 1988, 1999 by Tommy Nelson™, a division of Thomas Nelson, Inc. All rights reserved. Used by permission.

The Holman Christian Standard Bible™ (HCSB) Copyright © 1999, 2000, 2001 by Holman Bible Publishers. Used by permission.

Cover Design by Kim Russell / Wahoo Designs

Page Layout by Bart Dawsonn

ISBN 978-1-60587-093-9

Printed in the United States of America

KID DEVOS

ABOUT SELF-CONTROL

50 Devos

Kid
DEVOS

A Message to Parents

If your child's bookshelf is already spilling over with a happy assortment of good books for kids, congratulations—that means you're a thoughtful parent who understands the importance of reading to your child.

This book is an important addition to your child's library. It is intended to be read by Christian parents to their young children. The text contains 50 brief chapters. Each chapter consists of a Bible verse, a brief story or lesson, kid-friendly quotations from notable Christian thinkers, a tip, and a prayer. Every chapter examines a different aspect of an important Biblical theme: self-control.

For the next 50 days, take the time to read one chapter each night to your child, and then spend a few moments talking about the chapter's meaning. In doing so, you will have 50 different opportunities to share God's wisdom with your son or daughter, and that's good . . . very good.

If you have been touched by God's love and His grace, then you know the joy that He has brought into your own life. Now it's your turn to share His message with the boy or girl whom He has entrusted to your care. Happy reading! And may God richly bless you and your family now and forever.

Self-Control Means Looking Before You Leap

Trust the Lord with all your heart.
Don't depend on your own understanding.
Remember the Lord in everything you do.
And he will give you success.

Proverbs 3:5-6 ICB

Maybe you've heard this old saying: "Look before you leap." What does that saying mean? It means that you should stop and think before you do something. Otherwise, you might be sorry you did it.

Learning how to control yourself is an important part of growing up. The more you learn about self-control, the better. Self-control will help you at home, at school, and at church. That's why parents and teachers are happy to talk about the rewards of good self-control. And that's why you should be excited about learning how important it is to look before you leap . . . not after!

The alternative to discipline is disaster.

Vance Havner

A Parent's Tip!

If you expect your child to have self-control, then you must have it, too. When it comes to parenting, you can't really teach it if you won't really live it.

A Kid's Tip!

Think ahead: Before you do something, ask yourself this question: "Will I be ashamed if my parents find out?" If the answer to that question is "Yes," don't do it!

Today's Prayer

Dear Lord, sometimes I make mistakes.
When I do, forgive me. And help me,
Lord, to learn from my mistakes so that
I can be a better person and a better
example to my friends and family.
Amen

Patience Please!

*Always be humble and gentle.
Be patient and accept each other
with love.*

Ephesians 4:2 ICB

Do you want to learn self-control? Then you must learn the art of being patient. The dictionary defines the word *patience* as "the ability to be calm, tolerant, and understanding." Here's what that means: the word "calm" means being in control of your emotions (not letting your emotions control you). The word "tolerant" means being kind and considerate to people who are different from you. And, the word "understanding" means being able to put yourself in another person's shoes.

If you can be calm, tolerant, and understanding, you will be the kind of person whose good deeds are a blessing to your family and friends. And that's exactly the kind of person that God wants you to be.

God is more patient with us than
we are with ourselves.

Max Lucado

A Parent's Tip!

Be patient with your child's impatience. Children are
supposed to be more impulsive than adults; after
all, they're still kids. So be understanding of your
child's limitations and understanding of his or her
imperfections.

A Kid's Tip!

What's good for you is good for them, too: If you
want others to be patient with you, then you should
treat them in the same way. That's the Golden Rule,
and it should be your rule, too!

Today's Prayer

Lord, sometimes I am not very patient.
Slow me down and calm me down.
Help me to think wisely and to act wisely.
Today and every day, help me to learn
the wisdom of patience.
Amen

Following Directions

In all your ways acknowledge him,
and he will make your paths straight.

Proverbs 3:6 NIV

Directions, directions, directions. It seems like somebody is always giving you directions: telling you where to go, how to behave, and what to do next. But sometimes all these directions can be confusing! How can you understand everything that everybody tells you? The answer, of course, is that you must pay careful attention to those directions . . . and that means listening.

To become a careful listener, here are some things you must do:
1. Don't talk when you're supposed to be listening (your ears work best when your mouth is closed);
2. Watch the person who's giving the directions (when your eyes and ears work together, it's easier to understand things);
3. If you don't understand something, ask a question (it's better to ask now than to make a mistake later).

Obedience is the outward expression
of your love of God.

Henry Blackaby

A Parent's Tip!

You don't have to haul your kid to a deserted island to have a meaningful conversation. Meaningful moments between you and your child can happen anywhere—and it's up to you to make sure that they do.

A Kid's Tip!

If you're afraid to raise your hand and ask a question about a direction, remember this . . . if you don't understand something, lots of other people in the classroom probably don't understand it, either. So you'll be doing everybody a big favor if you raise your hand and ask your question.

Today's Prayer

Dear Lord, let me listen carefully to my
parents, to my teachers, and to You.
When I listen, I learn. Let me become
a better listener today than I was
yesterday, and let me become
an even better listener tomorrow.
Amen

Because It's What God Wants

Not My will, but Yours, be done.
Luke 22:42 HCSB

How much does God love you? He loves you so much that He sent His Son Jesus to come to this earth for you! And, when you accept Jesus into your heart, God gives you a gift that is more precious than gold: that gift is called "eternal life," which means that you will live forever with God in heaven!

God's love is bigger and more powerful than anybody can imagine, but it is very real. So do yourself a favor right now: accept God's love with open arms and welcome His Son Jesus into your heart. When you do, your life will be changed today, tomorrow, and forever.

And because we know Christ is alive,
we have hope for the present and hope for life
beyond the grave.

Billy Graham

A Parent's Tip!

Of course we know that God watches over us, but
we must also make certain that our children know
that we know. And, we must behave in ways that
let our children know that we know that He knows.
Whew!

A Kid's Tip!

Self-control Every Day: Self-control should be part
of our lives every day, not just on the days when
we feel good. God loves us every day and we should
obey Him every day. And remember: good behavior
starts with you, but if you're a good example to
others, it won't end there!

Today's Prayer

Dear Lord, thank You for watching
over me. Help me understand
what's right and do what's right,
today and always.
Amen

Listen to Your Conscience

*They show that in their hearts
they know what is right and wrong.*

Romans 2:15 ICB

God gave you something called a conscience: some people describe it as a little voice, but really, it's a feeling—it's a feeling that tells you whether something is right or wrong. Your conscience will usually tell you what to do and when to do it. Pay attention to that feeling, and trust it.

If you slow down and listen to your conscience, you'll usually stay out of trouble. And if you listen to your conscience, it won't be so hard to control your own behavior. Why? Because most of the time, your conscience already knows right from wrong. So don't be in such a hurry to do things. Instead of "jumping right in," listen to your conscience. In the end, you'll be very glad you did.

A quiet conscience sleeps in thunder.

Thomas Fuller

A Parent's Tip!

Sometimes, the little voice that we hear in our heads can be the echoes of our own parents' voices . . . and now that we're parents ourselves, we're the ones whose words will echo down through the hearts and minds of future generations. It's a big responsibility, but with God's help, we'll be up to the challenge.

A Kid's Tip!

If you're not sure what to do . . . trust your conscience. It's almost always right!

Today's Prayer

Dear Lord, You have given me
a conscience that tells me what is
right and what is wrong. I will listen to
that quiet voice so I can do
the right thing today and every day.
Amen

The Golden Rule

*This royal law is found in the Scriptures:
"Love your neighbor as yourself."
If you obey this law,
then you are doing right.*

James 2:8 ICB

When we learn how to control ourselves, we can be more considerate of other people. Would you like to make the world a better place? If so, you can start by practicing the Golden Rule.

Jesus said, "Do to others what you want them to do to you" (Matthew 7:12 NCV). That means that you should treat other people in the very same way that you want to be treated. That's the Golden Rule.

Jesus wants us to treat other people with respect, kindness, courtesy, and love. When we do, we make our families and friends happy . . . and we make our Father in heaven very proud. So if you want to know how to treat other people, ask the person you see every time you look into the mirror. The answer you receive will tell you exactly what to do.

Anything done for another is done for oneself.

Pope John Paul II

A Parent's Tip!

Make it your rule, too! When you become a living, breathing example of the Golden Rule in action, your child will notice, and the results will be better than gold.

A Kid's Tip!

How would you feel? When you're trying to decide how to treat another person, ask yourself this question: "How would I feel if somebody treated me that way?" Then, treat the other person the way that you would want to be treated.

Today's Prayer

Dear Lord, help me always to do my very best to treat others as I wish to be treated. The Golden Rule is Your rule, Father; let me also make it mine.

Amen

What the Bible Says

*Your word is like a lamp for my feet
and a light for my way.*

Psalm 119:105 ICB

What book contains everything that God has to say about self-control? The Bible, of course. If you read the Bible every day, you'll soon be convinced that self-control is very important to God. And, since doing the right thing (and the smart thing) is important to your Father in heaven, it should be important to you, too.

The Bible is the most important book you'll ever own. It's God's Holy Word. Read it every day, and follow its instructions. When you do, you'll be safe now and forever.

If we neglect the Bible, we cannot expect
to benefit from the wisdom and direction that
result from knowing God's Word.

Vonette Bright

A Parent's Tip!

How can you teach your children the importance of
God's Holy Word? By example. When teaching your
child about the Bible, words are fine—but actually
living the Bible is far better.

A Kid's Tip!

Read the Bible? Every Day!: Try to read your Bible
with your parents every day. If they forget, remind
them!

Today's Prayer

Dear Lord, the Bible is Your gift to me.
Let me use, let me trust it,
and let me obey it,
today and every day that I live.
Amen

You Don't Have to Go Along with the Crowd

Do you think I am trying to make people accept me? No, God is the One am trying to please. Am I trying to please people? If I still wanted to please people, I would not be a servant of Christ.

Galatians 1:10 NCV

It happens to all of us at one time or another: a friend asks us to do something that we think is wrong. What should we do? Should we try to please our friend by doing something bad? No way! It's not worth it!

Trying to please our friends is okay. What's not okay is misbehaving in order to do so.

Do you have a friend who encourages you to misbehave? Hopefully you don't have any friends like that. But if you do, say, "No, NO, NOOOOOO!" And what if your friend threatens to break up the friendship? Let him! Friendships like that just aren't worth it.

Those who follow the crowd usually get lost in it.

Rick Warren

A Parent's Tip!

Be a good example: If you are burdened with a "people-pleasing" personality, outgrow it. Realize that you can't please all of the people all of the time (including your children), nor should you attempt to.

A Kid's Tip!

Face facts: since you can't please everybody, you're better off trying to please the people who are trying to help you become a better person, not the people who are encouraging you to misbehave!

Today's Prayer

Dear Lord, there's a right way
and a wrong way to do things.
Let me do what's right and keep doing
what's right every day of my life.
Amen

Slowing Down Long Enough to Listen

Wise people can also listen and learn.

Proverbs 1:5 NCV

When God made you, He gave you two ears and one mouth for a very good reason: you can learn at least twice as much by listening as you can by talking. That's why it's usually better to listen first and talk second. But when you're frustrated or tired, it's easy to speak first and think later.

A big part of growing up is learning how to slow down long enough to listen to the things that people have to say. So the next time you're tempted to turn off your ears and tune up your mouth, stop, listen, and think. After all, God gave you two wonderful ears for a very good reason: to use them.

One of the best ways to encourage someone who's hurting is with your ears—by listening.

Barbara Johnson

A Parent's Tip!

Great communicators listen first and speak second; poor communicators complete the same tasks, but in reverse order.

A Kid's Tip!

Listening Shows You Care: When you listen to the things other people have to say, it shows that you care about their message and about them. Listening carefully is not just the courteous thing to do, it's also the kind thing to do.

Today's Prayer

Dear Lord, I have lots to learn.
Help me to watch, to listen, to think,
and to learn, every day of my life.
Amen

Knowing Right from Wrong . . . and Doing It!

Praise the Lord! Happy are those who respect the Lord, who want what he commands.

Psalm 112:1 NCV

If you're old enough to know right from wrong, then you're old enough to do something about it. In other words, you should always try to do the right thing, and you should also do your very best not to do the wrong thing.

The more self-control you have, the easier it is to do the right thing. Why? Because, when you learn to think first and do things next, you avoid lots of silly mistakes. So here's great advice: first, slow down long enough to figure out the right thing to do—and then do it. You'll make yourself happy, and you'll make lots of other people happy, too.

Obedience to God is our job.

Elisabeth Elliot

A Parent's Tip!

Obedience begins at home. If your children don't learn obedience between the four walls of your home, they probably won't learn it anywhere else.

A Kid's Tip!

When in doubt, ask mom or dad: If you're not sure whether something is right or wrong, ask your parents before you do it!

Today's Prayer

Dear Lord, when I'm tempted to do
the wrong thing, help me to slow down
and to think about my behavior.
And then, help me to know what's right
and to do what's right.
Amen

Parents Can Help

Honor your father and your mother.

Exodus 20:12 ICB

Whenever you want to get better at something, you should always be willing to let your parents help out in any way they can. After all, your parents want you to become the very best person you can be. So, if you want to become better at controlling your own behavior, ask your parents to help. How can they help out? By reminding you to slow down and think about things before you do them—not after. It's as simple as that.

The child that never learns to obey
his parents in the home will not obey God
or man out of the home.

Susanna Wesley

A Parent's Tip!

Hey Mom and Dad, how do you treat your parents?
If you're lucky enough to have parents who are
living, remember that the way you treat them is the
way you're training your kids to treat you.

A Kid's Tip!

Calm down . . . sooner rather than later! If you're
angry with a friend or family member, don't blurt
out something unkind. If you can't say anything nice,
go to your room and don't come out until you can.

Today's Prayer

Dear Lord, You have given me a family
that cares for me and loves me.
Thank You. Let me love everybody in
my family, even when they're not
perfect. And let me always be thankful
that my family loves me even when
I'm not perfect.
Amen

Safety First

*Innocent people will be kept safe.
But those who are dishonest will
suddenly be ruined.*

Proverbs 28:18 ICB

Self-control and safety go hand in hand. Why? Because a big part of self-control is looking around and thinking things through before you do something that you might regret later.

Remember the saying "Look before you leap!"? Well if you want to live safely and happily, you should look very carefully before you decide whether or not to leap. After all, it's easy to leap, but once you're in the middle of your jump, it's too late to leap back!

Waiting is an essential part of spiritual discipline.

Anne Graham Lotz

A Parent's Tip!

Talk It Over: If your child has done something that is impulsive, discourteous, or dangerous, your natural response will be anger. But as soon as you calm down, help your child learn from the experience by talking about the behavior, its motivations, and its consequences.

A Kid's Tip!

Don't complain about safety: whether it's a fire drill at school or wearing seat belts in the family car, don't whine, complain, or resist. When grown-ups are trying to keep you safe, your job is to help them do it!

Today's Prayer

Dear Lord, You protect me;
help me to learn how to protect myself.
Help me to slow down, to think ahead,
and to look before I leap. You are
concerned with my safety, Lord.
Help me to be concerned with it, too.
Amen

When the Teacher Isn't Looking

*The honest person will live safely,
but the one who is dishonest
will be caught.*

Proverbs 10:9 ICB

When your teachers or parents aren't watching, what should you do? The answer, of course, is that you should behave exactly like you would if they were watching you. But sometimes, you may be tempted to do otherwise.

When a parent steps away or a teacher looks away, you may be tempted to say something or do something that you would not do if they were standing right beside you. But remember this: when nobody's watching, it's up to you to control yourself. And that's exactly everybody wants you to do: your teachers want you to control yourself, and so do your parents. And so, by the way, does God.

Character is what you are in the dark.

D. L. Moody

A Parent's Tip!

Some families stress the importance of education more than other families. Make yours a home in which the importance of education is clearly a high priority.

A Kid's Tip!

Behavior you can be proud of: When teachers or parents aren't looking, it's up to you to control yourself. So think about what you're doing, and think about the consequences of your behavior.

Today's Prayer

Dear Lord, sometimes it's easier to misbehave than it is to slow down and think about the best way to behave. But even when doing the right thing is difficult, let me slow down long enough to think about the right thing to say or do.

Amen

The Rewards
of Self-Control

*So prepare your minds for service
and have self-control.*

1 Peter 1:13 NCV

Who needs to learn more about self-control? You do! Why? Well, for one thing, you'll discover that good things happen to people (like you) who are wise enough to think ahead and smart enough to look before they leap.

Whether you're at home or at school, you'll learn that the best rewards go to the kids who control their behavior—not to the people who let their behaviors control them!

Nobody is good by accident.
No man ever became holy by chance.

C. H. Spurgeon

A Parent's Tip!

Parents make the best encouragers! You're not just
your children's parents, you're their biggest fans.
Make sure they know it.

A Kid's Tip!

Use the Golden Rule to help you decide what to say
and how to behave: Treat people like you want to be
treated!

Today's Prayer

Dear Lord, You have given me so many blessings, and You want to give me even more. Thank You. Here's how I will show my thanks: I will use my talents and I will behave myself.

Amen

Stop, Look, and Think!

A wise person is patient.

Proverbs 19:11 ICB

The Book of Proverbs tells us that self-control and patience are very good things to have. But for most of us, self-control and patience can also be very hard things to learn.

Are you having trouble being patient? And are you having trouble slowing down long enough to think before you act? If so, remember that self-control takes practice, and lots of it, so keep trying. And if you make a mistake, don't be too upset. After all, if you're going to be a really patient person, you shouldn't just be patient with others; you should also be patient with yourself.

Teach us, O Lord, the disciplines of patience,
for to wait is often harder than to work.

Peter Marshall

A Parent's Tip!

It's always a good time to put the brakes on
impulsive behavior . . . theirs and yours!

A Kid's Tip!

Stop, think, then speak: If you want to make your
words useful instead of hurtful, don't open your
mouth until you've turned on your brain!

Today's Prayer

Dear Lord, let me be patient with other people's mistakes. And let me be patient with my own. I know that I still have so many things to learn. I won't stop learning, I won't give up, and I won't stop growing up. Every day, I will do my best to become a little bit more like the person You intend for me to be.

Amen

Learning Lessons from Our Mistakes . . . the First Time

A wise person pays attention to correction that will improve his life.

Proverbs 15:31 ICB

Do you ever make mistakes? Of course you do . . . everybody does. And when you make a mistake, it's not so terrible if you learn something. Why should you try to learn from your mistakes? So you won't make the very same mistakes again.

When you have done things that you regret, you should apologize, you should clean up the mess you've made, you should learn from your mistakes, and—last but not least—you should forgive yourself. Mistakes happen . . . it's simply a fact of life, and it's simply a part of growing up. So don't be too hard on yourself, especially if you've learned something along the way.

Father, take our mistakes and turn them
into opportunities.

Max Lucado

A Parent's Tip!

Kids learn by example. So how can you teach your
child to forgive himself when he makes a mistake?
By forgiving yourself when you make one.

A Kid's Tip!

Made a mistake? Ask for forgiveness? If you've
broken one of God's rules, you can always ask Him
for His forgiveness. And He will always give it!

Today's Prayer

Dear Lord, sometimes I make mistakes.
When I do, help me learn something,
help me forgive myself, and help me
become a smarter person today
than I was yesterday.
Amen

Don't Give Up

*We must not become tired
of doing good.*

Galatians 6:2 ICB

If you're having trouble learning how to control your actions or your emotions, you're not alone! Most people have problems with self-control from time to time, so don't be discouraged. Just remember that self-control requires practice and lots of it. So if you're a little discouraged, don't give up. Just keep working on improving your self-control until you get better at it. . . . and if you keep trying, you can be sure that sooner or later, you will get better at it.

Keep adding, keep walking, keep advancing;
do not stop, do not turn back,
do not turn from the straight road.

St. Augustine

A Parent's Tip!

Remember the advice of Winston Churchill: He said, "Never give in; never give in; never give in." And that's good advice whether you're leading a nation or a family.

A Kid's Tip!

Everybody is a VIP: VIP means "Very Important Person." To God, everybody is a VIP, and we should treat every person with dignity, patience, and respect.

Today's Prayer

Dear Lord, help me to make Your world
a better place. I can't fix all the world's
troubles, but I can help make things
better with kind words, good deeds,
and sincere prayers. Let my actions
and my prayers be pleasing to You, Lord,
now and forever.
Amen

Pray About It!

Always be happy. Never stop praying.
Give thanks whatever happens.
That is what God wants for you
in Christ Jesus.

1 Thessalonians: 5:16-18 ICB

Do you really want to become a more patient person? Then pray about it. Would you like to learn how to use better self-control? Then pray about it. If you are upset, pray about it. If there is something you're worried about, ask God to comfort you. And as you pray more, you'll discover that God is always near and that He's always ready to hear from you. So don't worry about things; pray about them. God is waiting . . . and listening!

Prayer accomplishes more than anything else.

Bill Bright

A Parent's Tip!

Are you embarrassed to bow your head in a restaurant? Don't be; it's the people who aren't praying who should be embarrassed!

A Kid's Tip!

Pray early and often: One way to make sure that your heart is in tune with God is to pray often. The more you talk to God, the more He will talk to you.

Today's Prayer

Dear Lord, help me remember
the importance of prayer.
You always hear my prayers, God;
let me always pray them!
Amen

Homework

Remember what you are taught.
And listen carefully to words
of knowledge.

Proverbs 23:12 ICB

Sooner or later, you'll start getting homework, and when that day comes, you'd better be ready because that's when you'll really need lots of self-control! Usually, homework isn't hard to do, but it takes time. And sometimes, we'd rather be doing other things (like playing outside or watching TV). But, when we put off our homework until the last possible minute, we make it hard on ourselves.

Instead of putting off your homework, do it first. Then, you'll have the rest of your time to have fun—and you won't have to worry about all that homework.

Not now becomes never.

Martin Luther

A Parent's Tip!

Teach by example. Whatever "it" is, do it now. When you do, you'll demonstrate to your child the value of doing things sooner rather than later.

A Kid's Tip!

The habit of putting things off . . . is a habit that you're better off without.

Today's Prayer

Dear Lord, You have given me
a wonderful gift: time here on earth.
Let me use it wisely today
and every day that I live.
Amen

Quiet Please

In quietness and trust is your strength.

Isaiah 30:15 NASB

Have you learned how to sit quietly and listen to your parents and your teachers? Have you learned how to listen respectfully—with your ears open wide and your mouth closed tight? If so, give yourself a big pat on the back (or if you can't reach way back there, ask your mom or dad to do it for you!).

An important part of learning self-control is learning how to be quiet when you're supposed to be quiet. It isn't always easy, but the sooner you learn how to sit quietly and behave respectfully, the better. So you might as well start today.

A quiet time is a basic ingredient
in a maturing relationship with God.

Charles Stanley

A Parent's Tip!

Silence is okay: Sometimes, just being there is enough. If you're not sure what to say, it's okay to say nothing.

A Kid's Tip!

And when you speak, be respectful to everybody, starting with parents, grandparents, teachers, and adults . . . but don't stop there. Be respectful of everybody, including yourself!

Today's Prayer

Dear Lord, let me listen respectfully to
my parents, to my teachers, and to You.
I have much to learn. Let me learn as
much as I can as soon as I can,
and let me be a good example
for other people to follow.
Amen

Parents Are Smarter Than You Think

*My child, listen to your father's teaching.
And do not forget your mother's advice.*

Proverbs 1:8 ICB

Do you listen carefully to the things your parents tell you? You should. Your parents want the very best for you. They want you to be happy and healthy; they want you to be smart and to do smart things. Your parents have much to teach you, and you have much to learn. So listen carefully to the things your mom and dad have to say. And ask lots of questions. When you do, you'll soon discover that your parents have lots of answers . . . lots of very good answers.

Perfect parents don't exist,
but a perfect God does.

Beth Moore

A Parent's Tip!

Have a few important rules . . . and enforce them:
No matter how big your children are, they still need
to abide by your rules if they want to reside under
your roof.

A Kid's Tip!

Talking versus Really Talking: Don't be too
embarrassed or too fearful to tell your parents
what you're really thinking about. They understand
more than you think they do!

Today's Prayer

Lord, let me be respectful of all people,
starting with my family and friends.
And, let me share the love that
I feel in my heart with them . . .
and with You!
Amen

No More Tantrums

Do not become angry easily.
Anger will not help you live a good life
as God wants.

James 1:19 ICB

Temper tantrums are one of the silliest ways to lose self-control. Why? Because when we lose our temper, we say things that we shouldn't say, and we do things that we shouldn't do. And to make matters worse, once the tantrum is over, we usually feel embarrassed or worse. Too bad!

The Bible tells us that it is usually foolish to become angry and that it is wise to remain calm. That's why we should learn to control our tempers before our tempers control us.

Life is too short to spend it being
angry, bored, or dull.

Barbara Johnson

A Parent's Tip!

When your child becomes upset, you'll be tempted
to become upset, too. Resist that temptation.
Remember that in a house-full of kids and grown-
ups, you're the grown-up. And it's up to you to
remain calm even when other, less mature members
of the family can't.

A Kid's Tip!

Think carefully . . . make that very carefully! If
you're a little angry, think carefully before you
speak. If you're very angry, think very carefully.
Otherwise, you might say something mean that you'll
be sorry you said.

Today's Prayer

Dear Lord, help me to turn away from
angry thoughts and angry people.
Help me always to use Jesus as my guide
for life, and let me trust His promises
today and forever.
Amen

Being an Example to Others

You are the light that gives light to the world . . . . In the same way, you should be a light for other people. Live so that they will see the good things you do and will praise your Father in heaven.

Matthew 5:14, 16 NCV

What kind of example are you? Are you the kind of person who shows other people what it means to be well behaved? And, are you learning to use more and more self-control? Hopefully so!!!

Whether you realize it or not, you're an example to your friends and family members. So today, be a good example for others to follow. Because God needs people (like you) who are willing to behave themselves as God intends. And that's exactly the kind of example you should try to be.

A good example is the best sermon.

Thomas Fuller

A Parent's Tip!

Give your children the gift of a lifetime. How? By being a worthy example—practice what you preach.

A Kid's Tip!

Look around! Someone very near you may need a helping hand or a kind word, so keep your eyes open, and look for people who need your help, whether at home, at church, or at school.

Today's Prayer

Lord, make me a worthy example to my
family and friends. And, let my words
and my deeds serve as a testimony to
the changes You have made in my life.
Let me praise You, Father, by following
in the footsteps of Your Son,
and let others see Him through me.
Amen

Listen . . . and Obey

Lord, teach me your demands,
and I will keep them until the end.

Psalm 119:33 NCV

When you learn to control your actions and your words, you will find it easier to obey your parents, your teachers, and your Father in heaven. Why? Because in order to be an obedient person, you must first learn how to control yourself—otherwise, you won't be able to obey very well, even when you want to.

When you learn the importance of obedience, you'll soon discover that good things happen when you behave yourself. And the sooner you learn to listen and obey, the sooner those good things will start happening.

Let us trust God's promises
and obey His commandments.

John Calvin

A Parent's Tip!

Every family puts something or someone in first place. Does God occupy first place in your family? If so, congratulations! If not, it's time to reorder your priorities.

A Kid's Tip!

Obeying God? Yes! What about the rules you learn about in the Bible? Well, those aren't just any old rules—they're God's rules. And you should behave—and obey—accordingly.

Today's Prayer

Dear Lord, You know what's best for me.
I will study Your Word and obey
Your teachings this day and forever.
Amen

Learning to Wait Your Turn

Patience is better than power.

Proverbs 16:32 HCSB

When we're standing in line or waiting our turn, it's tempting to push ahead of other people. And it's tempting to scream, "Me first!", but it's the wrong thing to do! The Bible tells us that we shouldn't push ahead of others; instead, we should do the right thing—and the polite thing—by saying, "You first!"

Sometimes, waiting your turn can be hard, especially if you're excited or in a hurry. But even then, waiting patiently is the right thing to do. Why? Because parents say so, teachers say so, and, most importantly, God says so!

Patience is the companion of wisdom.

St. Augustine

A Parent's Tip!

When it comes to courteous behavior, you are your child's most important role model. So pay careful attention to the way that you treat other people, especially those who are not in a position to help you. For further instructions, read Matthew 25:40.

A Kid's Tip!

God and your parents have been patient with you . . . now it's your turn to be patient with others.

Today's Prayer

Lord, sometimes it's hard to be
a patient person, and that's exactly when
I should try my hardest to be patient.
Help me to be patient and kind,
even when it's hard.
Amen

What It Means to Be Wise

Wisdom begins with respect for the Lord.

Proverbs 9:10 ICB

If you look in a dictionary, you'll see that the word "wisdom" means "using good judgement, and knowing what is true," But there's more: it's not just enough to know what's right; if you really want to become a wise person, you must also do what's right.

A big part of "doing what's right" is learning self-control . . . and the best day to start learning self-control is this one!

Wisdom enlarges our capacity for discovery and delight, causing wonder to grow as we grow.

Susan Lenzkes

A Parent's Tip!

Need wisdom? God's got it. If you want it, then study God's Word and associate with godly people.

A Kid's Tip!

Learning about Jesus: Start learning about Jesus, and keep learning about Him as long as you live. His story never grows old, and His teachings never fail.

Today's Prayer

Dear Lord, I trust Your wisdom.
The most important wisdom is Yours
and the most important truth is Yours.
Today, I will show my respect for You
by obeying Your commandments.
Amen

If You're Not Sure What to Do

*The Lord says, "I will make you wise
and show you where to go.
I will guide you and watch over you."*
Psalm 32:8 NCV

When you're not sure whether something is right or wrong, ask yourself a simple question: "How would Jesus behave if He were here?" The answer to that question will tell you what to do.

Jesus was perfect, but we are not. Still, we must try as hard as we can to do the best that we can. When we do, we will love others, just as Christ loves us.

God's Word is a light not only to our path
but also to our thinking. Place it in your heart today,
and you will never walk in darkness.

Joni Eareckson Tada

A Parent's Tip!

Be a parent first and a friend second. As your child
grows into adulthood, you'll be tempted to become
"one of the boys" (or girls). Resist that temptation.
Remember that your kid has lots of friends but
only a couple of parents. So whatever you do, don't
abandon your paternal responsibilities . . . your child
needs a parent more than a pal.

A Kid's Tip!

When in doubt: do the thing that you think Jesus
would do. And, of course, don't do something if you
think that He wouldn't do it.

Today's Prayer

Dear Lord, even when I don't understand
why things happen, I will trust You.
Even when I am confused or worried,
I will trust You. There are many things
that I cannot do, Lord, and there are
many things that I cannot understand.
But one thing I can do is to
trust You always. And I will.

Amen

You'll Be Happier

Happy is the person who . . .
loves what the Lord commands.

Psalm 112:1 ICB

Do you want to be happy? Here are some things you should do: Love God and His Son, Jesus; obey the Golden Rule; learn how to control yourself, and always try to do what you think is right. When you do these things, you'll discover that happiness goes hand-in-hand with good behavior.

The happiest people do not misbehave; the happiest people are not cruel or thoughtless. The happiest people don't say unkind things. The happiest people are those who love God and follow His rules—starting, of course, with the Golden one.

When we bring sunshine into the lives of others,
we're warmed by it ourselves.
When we spill a little happiness, it splashes on us.

Barbara Johnson

A Parent's Tip!

Your children deserve to grow up in a happy home . . .
and you owe it to them (and to yourself) to provide
that kind of home.

A Kid's Tip!

Better self-control can help make you happy: the
better you behave, the more fun you'll have. And
don't let anybody try to tell you otherwise.

Today's Prayer

Dear Lord, I am thankful for all
the blessings You have given me.
Let me be a happy Christian, Father,
as I share Your joy with friends,
with family, and with the world.
Amen

When Nobody Is Around

*Good people will be guided by honesty;
dishonesty will destroy those
who are not trustworthy.*

Proverbs 11:3 NCV

Even when nobody's watching, God is. And He knows whether you've done the right thing or the wrong thing. So if you're tempted to misbehave when nobody is looking, remember this: There is never a time when "nobody's watching." Somebody is always watching over you—and that Somebody, of course, is your Father in heaven. Don't let Him down!

Integrity is a sign of maturity.

Charles Swindoll

A Parent's Tip!

If your child tells a falsehood, talk about it. Even "little white lies" are worthy of a parent-to-child talk; the bigger the lie, the bigger the talk.

A Kid's Tip!

Want something? Ask, don't take! It's okay to ask. It's not okay to take!

Today's Prayer

Dear Lord, help me to behave myself like
a good Christian! Let me keep Christ in
my heart, and let me put the devil
in his place: far away from me!
Amen

When in Doubt, Slow Down

Step out of the traffic!
Take a long, loving look at me,
your High God, above politics,
above everything.

Psalm 46:10 MSG

Maybe you're one of those people who try to do everything fast, faster, or fastest! If so, maybe you sometimes do things before you think about the consequences of your actions. If that's the case, it's probably a good idea to slow down a little bit so you can think before you act. When you do, you'll soon discover the value of thinking carefully about things before you get started. And while you're at it, it's probably a good idea to think before you speak, too. After all, you'll never have to apologize for something that you didn't say.

You can always go to God with your questions.
You may not find all the answers, but in finding God,
you know the One who does.

Max Lucado

A Parent's Tip!

You know that "God is love." Now, it's your
responsibility to make certain that your children
know it, too.

A Kid's Tip!

Got Questions? If you're faced with too many
questions and too few answers, slow down, and talk
to your parents. When you do, you'll discover that
your parents probably have more answers than you
have questions.

Today's Prayer

Dear Lord, sometimes this world can be a puzzling place. When I am unsure what to do, let me be quick to learn from my parents, and let me be quick to learn from You.

Amen

Picking the Right Words to Say

Don't use foul or abusive language.
Let everything you say be good and
helpful, so that your words will be
an encouragement to those
who hear them.

Ephesians 4:29 NLT

Have you learned to control the words you speak? Hopefully so. After all, your words have the power to help other people. And, since you want other folks to say kind things to you, you should say kind things to them, too.

So make certain that you're a person who says helpful things, not hurtful things. You'll feel better about yourself when you help other people feel better about themselves. Everybody needs to hear kind words, and that's exactly the kind of words they should hear from you!

Change the heart, and you change the speech.

Warren Wiersbe

A Parent's Tip!

Parents set the boundaries: Whether they realize it or not, parents (not kids) establish the general tone of the conversations that occur within their homes. And it's up to parents to ensure that the tone of those conversations is a tone that's pleasing to God.

A Kid's Tip!

Think before you speak: If you want to keep from hurting other people's feelings, don't open your mouth until you've turned on your brain.

Today's Prayer

Dear Lord, I will try to show respect to everybody, starting with my family and my friends. And, I will do my best to share the love that I feel in my heart for them . . . and for You!

Amen

Self-control Equals Happiness

When people do not accept
divine guidance, they run wild.
But whoever obeys the law is happy.

Proverbs 29:18 NLT

Do you want to be happy? Then you should learn to obey your parents and your teachers. And, of course, you should also learn to obey God. When you do, you'll discover that happiness goes hand-in-hand with good behavior.

The happiest people do not misbehave; the happiest people are not cruel or greedy. The happiest people don't disobey their parents, their teachers, or their Father in heaven. The happiest people are those who obey the rules . . .

And it's up to you to make sure that you're one of those happy people.

The surest evidence of our love to Christ is
obedience to the laws of Christ.
Love is the root, obedience is the fruit.

Matthew Henry

A Parent's Tip!

Teaching Them Obedience: Your children will learn
about life from many sources; the most important
source should be you. But remember that the
lectures you give are never as important as the ones
you live.

A Kid's Tip!

Learning how to obey makes you a better person.
You have many teachers. Listen to them and obey
them. When you do, you'll become a better person.

Today's Prayer

Dear Lord, I trust You, and I know
that Your rules are good for me.
I will do my best to obey You,
even when it's hard.
Amen

Self-control Means Being Honest

Doing what is right brings freedom to honest people.

Proverbs 11:6 ICB

Have you ever said something that wasn't true? When you did, were you sorry for what you had said? Probably so.

When we're dishonest, we make ourselves unhappy in surprising ways. Here are just a few troubles that result from dishonesty: we feel guilty and we are usually found out and we disappoint others and we disappoint God. It's easy to see that lies always cause more problems than they solve.

Happiness and honesty always go hand in hand. But it's up to you to make sure that you go hand in hand with them!

The single most important element in any human relationship is honesty—with oneself, with God, and with others.

Catherine Marshall

A Parent's Tip!

The truth can be hard for parents, too: telling the truth isn't just hard for kids. And when honesty is hard, that's precisely the moment when wise parents remember that their children are watching . . . and learning.

A Kid's Tip!

When telling the truth is hard . . . it probably means that you're afraid of what others might think—or what they might do—if you're truthful. But even when telling the truth is hard, it's always the right thing to do.

Today's Prayer

Dear Lord, sometimes it's hard to tell
the truth. But even when telling
the truth is difficult, let me follow
Your commandment. Honesty isn't just
the best policy, Lord; it's Your policy,
and I will obey You by making it
my policy, too.
Amen

Respecting Authority

Show respect for all people.
Love the brothers and sisters
of God's family.

1 Peter 2:17 ICB

Are you polite and respectful to your parents and teachers? And do you do your best to treat everybody with the respect they deserve? If you want to obey God's rules, then you should be able to answer yes to these questions.

Remember this: the Bible teaches you to be a respectful person—and if it's right there in the Bible, it's certainly the right thing to do!

He that will have his son have respect for him
and his orders must himself have
a great reverence for his son.

John Locke

A Parent's Tip!

The Golden Rule . . . is as good as gold—in fact, it's
better than gold. And as a responsible parent, you
should make certain that your child knows that the
Golden Rule is, indeed, golden.

A Kid's Tip!

Respecting all kinds of people: Make sure that you
show proper respect for everyone, even if that
person happens to be different from you. It's easy
to make fun of people who seem different . . . but
it's wrong.

Today's Prayer

Dear God, I pray for those who care
for me, especially my parents.
Give them wisdom, courage,
compassion, and faith.
Amen

Your Good Deeds

*A good person produces good deeds
from a good heart.*

Luke 6:45 NLT

It's a fact: sharing makes you a better person. Why? Because when you share, you're doing several things: first, you're obeying God; and, you're making your corner of the world a better place; and you're learning exactly what it feels like to be a generous, loving person.

When you share, you have the fun of knowing that your good deeds are making other people happy. When you share, you're learning how to become a better person. When you share, you're making things better for other people and for yourself. So do the right thing: share!

If we do good deeds, we must remember that
our strength to do them comes from God.
We can't rely on our own strength.

Pope St. Gregory the Great

A Parent's Tip!

Parental love in action . . . Of course it's good to tell
your kids how you feel about them, but that's not
enough. You should also show your children how you
feel with your good deeds and your kind words.

A Kid's Tip!

You must do more than talk about it: In order to be
a good person, you must do good things. So get busy!
The best time to do a good deed is as soon as you
can do it!

Today's Prayer

Dear Lord, let me help others in every
way that I can. Jesus served others;
I can too. I will serve other people
with my good deeds and with my prayers,
and I will give thanks for all those
who serve and protect
our nation and our world.
Amen

The Cheerful Giver

God loves a cheerful giver.

2 Corinthians 9:7 NIV

It takes maturity and self-control to share your things. When you learn how to share, you'll know that you've done exactly what God wants you to do—and you'll feel better about yourself, too.

The Bible teaches that it's better to be generous than selfish. But sometimes, you won't feel like sharing, and you'll be tempted to keep everything for yourself. When you're feeling a little bit stingy, remember this: God wants you to share your things with people who need your help.

When you learn to be a more generous person, God will be pleased with you . . . and you'll be pleased with yourself.

He climbs highest who helps another up.

Zig Ziglar

A Parent's Tip!

Good Samaritan 101: You're the teacher. Class is in session. Your child is in attendance. Actions speak louder than words. And it's one of the most important courses you will ever teach.

A Kid's Tip!

When are you old enough to start giving? If you're old enough to understand these words, you're old enough to start giving to your church and to those who are less fortunate than you. If you're not sure about the best way to do it, ask your parents!

Today's Prayer

Dear Lord, I know there is no happiness
in keeping Your blessings for myself.
Today, I will share my blessings with
my family, with my friends,
and people who need my help.
Amen

Learn About
Self-control
in Church

Don't you realize that all of you together
are the temple of God and that
the Spirit of God lives in you?

1 Corinthians 3:16 NLT

You can learn about self-control in church. When your parents take you to church, are you pleased to go? And once you get there, do you behave yourself? Hopefully so.

The church belongs to God just as surely as you belong to God. That's why the church is also a very good place to learn about God and about His Son Jesus.

So when your mom and dad take you to church, remember this: church is a fine place to be . . . and you're lucky to be there.

How beautiful it is to learn that grace isn't fragile,
and that in the family of God
we can fail and not be a failure.

Gloria Gaither

A Parent's Tip!

Make church a celebration, not an obligation: Your attitude towards church will help determine your kid's attitude toward church . . . so celebrate accordingly!

A Kid's Tip!

Forget the Excuses: If somebody starts making up reasons not to go to church, don't pay any attention . . . even if that person is you!

Today's Prayer

Dear Lord, thank You for my church.
When I am at church, I will be generous,
kind, well-behaved, and respectful.
And when I am not at church,
I will act the same way.
Amen

Making Good Decisions

Keep your eyes focused on what is right.
Keep looking straight ahead
to what is good.

Proverbs 4:25 ICB

Do you behave differently because you're a Christian? Or do you behave in pretty much the same way that you would if you had never heard of Jesus? Hopefully, you make better decisions because of the things you've learned from the Bible.

Doing the right thing is not always easy, especially when you're tired or frustrated. But, doing the wrong thing almost always leads to trouble. So here's some advice: remember the lessons you learn from the Bible. And keep remembering them every day of your life.

Successful people make right decisions
early and manage those decisions daily.

John Maxwell

A Parent's Tip!

It's not just important to teach your child what to
think. It's also important to teach your child how
to think (and there's a big difference between the
two).

A Kid's Tip!

Think ahead! Before you do something, ask yourself
this question: "Will I be ashamed if my parents find
out?" If the answer to that question is "Yes," don't
do it!

Today's Prayer

Dear Lord, there's a right way
to do things and a wrong way.
Help me to do things the right way
today and every day.
Amen

Put God First

Do not worship any other gods besides me.

Exodus 20:3 NLT

Are you willing to put God first, or do you put other things ahead of your love for Him? God wants you to love Him first, and He wants you to obey Him first. When you do these things, you'll be happy you did!

When the Pharisees quizzed Jesus about God's most important commandment, Jesus answered, "Love the Lord your God with all your heart, all your soul, and all your mind. This is the first and most important command" (Matthew 22:37-38 NCV). So if you want to do the right thing, always put Him in the place He deserves: first place.

God deserves first place in your life . . .
and you deserve the experience
of putting Him there.

Marie T. Freeman

A Parent's Tip!

Is He First in Your Family? Every family puts
something or someone in first place. Does
God occupy first place in your family? If so,
congratulations! If not, it's time to reorder your
priorities.

A Kid's Tip!

Talk to your parents about some of the ways you can
put God in first place.

Today's Prayer

Dear Lord, today I will put You first in
my thoughts, my actions,
and my prayers. I will seek to please You,
and I will strive to serve You.

Amen

Controlling Your Thoughts

Fix your thoughts on what is true and honorable and right. Think about things that are pure and lovely and admirable. Think about things that are excellent and worthy of praise.

Philippians 4:8 NLT

Do you try to think the kind of thoughts that make you happy, not sad? The Bible says that you should.

Do you try to think about things that are true and right? The Bible says that you should.

Do you turn away from bad thoughts—and away from people who misbehave? The Bible says that you should.

The Bible instructs you to guard your thoughts against things that are hurtful or wrong. So remember this: when you turn away from the bad thoughts and bad people, you've made a very wise choice.

People who do not develop and practice good
thinking often find themselves at the mercy
of their circumstances.

John Maxwell

A Parent's Tip!

If your thoughts tend toward the negative end of
the spectrum, redirect them. How? You can start by
counting your blessings and by thanking your Father
in heaven. And while you're at it, train yourself to
begin thinking thoughts that are more rational, more
accepting, and more upbeat . . . for everybody's
sake.

A Kid's Tip!

Good thoughts lead to good deeds and bad thoughts
lead elsewhere. So guard your thoughts accordingly.

Today's Prayer

Dear Lord, help me think about things
that are good, things that are true,
and things that are right . . .
starting right now!
Amen

Be Thankful!

Give thanks in all circumstances;
for this is God's will for you
in Christ Jesus.

1 Thessalonians 5:18 NIV

Do you have a thankful attitude? Hopefully so! After all, you've got plenty of things to be thankful for. Even during those times when you're angry or tired, you're a very lucky person.

Who has given you all the blessings you enjoy? Your parents are responsible, of course. But all of your blessings really start with God. That's why you should say "Thank You" to God many times each day. He's given you so much . . . so thank Him, starting now.

It is only with gratitude that life becomes rich.

Dietrich Bonhoeffer

A Parent's Tip!

Today, as you hug your child or kiss your spouse—or as you gaze upon a passing cloud or marvel at a glorious sunset—think of what God has done for you and yours. And, every time you notice a gift from the Giver of all things good, praise Him. His gifts are beyond understanding, and His love endures forever.

A Kid's Tip!

Two magic words: Thank you! Your parents will never get tired of hearing those two little words, and neither will your friends. And neither, for that matter, will God.

Today's Prayer

Dear Lord, You have given me so many
blessings, and You want to give me even
more. Thank You. Here's how I will show
my thanks: I will have a good attitude,
I will be kind to other people,
and I will behave myself.
Amen

You're Talented!

Do not neglect the gift that is in you.

1 Timothy 4:14 HCSB

Face facts: you've got very special talents, talents that have been given to you by God. So here's a question: will you find the self-control to use your talents . . . or not?

God wants you to use your talents to become a better person and a better Christian. And that's what you should want for yourself.

As you're trying to figure out exactly what you're good at, be sure and talk about it with your parents. They can help you decide how best to use and improve the gifts God has given you. And that's good because the best way to thank God for His gifts is to use them!

In the great orchestra we call life,
you have an instrument and a song, and you owe it
to God to play them both sublimely.

Max Lucado

A Parent's Tip!

Hidden talent and not-so-hidden fun: Of course you want to help your child discover his or her hidden—or not-so-hidden—talents. A good place to start is by helping your child discover the topics and activities that are the most fun. Today's child's play may become tomorrow's passionate pursuit.

A Kid's Tip!

If you want to get better at something, practice a little. If you want to be outstanding, practice a lot.

Today's Prayer

Lord, thank You for the talents You have
given me. I will treasure those talents,
and I will use them as I try my best
to walk in the footsteps of Your Son.
Amen

The Right Kind of Habits

Do not be fooled:
"Bad friends will ruin good habits."

1 Corinthians 15:33 NCV

Perhaps you've tried to become a more disciplined person, but you're still falling back into your old habits. If so, don't get discouraged. Instead, become even more determined to become the person God wants you to be.

If you trust God, and if you keep asking Him to help you change bad habits, He will help you make yourself into a new person. So, if at first you don't succeed, keep praying. If you keep asking, you'll eventually get the answers you need.

Since behaviors become habits,
make them work with you and not against you.

E. Stanley Jones

A Parent's Tip!

First you make your habits; then your habits make
you. So it's always a good time to think about the
kind of person your habits are making you.

A Kid's Tip!

Choose Your Habits Carefully: Habits are easier to
make than they are to break, so be careful!

Today's Prayer

Dear Lord, help me form good habits.
And let me make a habit of sharing
the things that I own and the love
that I feel in my heart.
Amen

Guard Your Heart

As a face is reflected in water,
so the heart reflects the person.

Proverbs 27:19 NLT

You are near and dear to God. He loves you more than you can imagine, and He wants the very best for you. And one more thing: God wants you to guard your heart.

Every day, you are faced with choices . . . lots of them. You can do the right thing, or not. You can tell the truth, or not. You can be kind and generous and obedient. Or not.

Your mind and your heart will usually tell you the right thing to do. And if you listen to your parents and grandparents, they will help you, too, by teaching you God's rules. Then, you will learn that doing the right thing is always better than doing the wrong thing. And, by obeying God's rules, you will guard your heart by giving it to His Son Jesus.

To lose heart is to lose everything.

John Eldredge

A Parent's Tip!

God is holy and wants you to be holy. You should make certain that God's love is in your heart and you are obedient to Him.

A Kid's Tip!

God is holy and wants you to be holy. Christ died to make you holy. Make sure that your response to Christ's sacrifice is worthy of Him.

Today's Prayer

Dear Lord, You know my heart.
Help me to say things,
to do things, and to think things
that are pleasing to You.
Amen

Kindness Starts with You

Don't push your way to the front; don't sweet-talk your way to the top. Put yourself aside, and help others get ahead. Don't be obsessed with getting your own advantage. Forget yourselves long enough to lend a helping hand.

Philippians 2:3-4 MSG

If you're waiting for other people to be nice to you before you're nice to them, you've got it backwards. Kindness starts with you! You see, you can never control what other people will say or do, but you can control your own behavior.

The Bible tells us that we should never stop doing good deeds as long as we live. Kindness is God's way, and it should be our way, too.

Showing kindness to others is one of
the nicest things we can do for ourselves.

Janette Oke

A Parent's Tip!

Kindness is contagious; kids can catch it from their
parents.

A Kid's Tip!

Kind Is as Kind Does: In order to be a kind person,
you must do kind things. Thinking about them isn't
enough. So get busy! Your family and friends need
all the kindness they can get!

Today's Prayer

Lord, it's easy to be kind to some people
and difficult to be kind to others.
Let me be kind to all people
so that I might follow in
the footsteps of Your Son.
Amen

Big Things in Store...
For YOU!

Lord our God, treat us well.
Give us success in what we do;
yes, give us success in what we do.

Psalm 90:17 NCV

God makes this promise: If you have faith in Him, you can do BIG things! So if you have something important to do, pray about it and ask God for help. When you ask God to help you, He will. And while you're at it, never be afraid to ask your parents for help.

When you talk things over with your parents, you'll soon discover that they want you to do BIG things . . . and they can give you LOTS of help.

Success or failure can be pretty well predicted by
the degree to which the heart is fully in it.

John Eldredge

A Parent's Tip!

How do you define success? If you're wise, you
define it in accordance with God's Word.

A Kid's Tip!

Don't let others define success for you. That's
between you and God.

Today's Prayer

Dear Lord, let Your priorities be
my priorities. Let Your will be my will.
Let Your Word be my guide, and keep me
mindful that genuine success is a result,
not of the world's approval,
but of Your approval.

Amen

Controlling Your Attitude ... And Pleasing God

Therefore, whether we are at home or away, we make it our aim to be pleasing to Him.

2 Corinthians 5:9 HCSB

Are you interested in pleasing God? Are you interested in pleasing your parents? Your teachers? And your friends? If so, try to make your attitude the best it can be. When you try hard to have a good attitude, you'll make other people feel better—and you'll make yourself feel better, too.

God knows everything about you, including your attitude. And when your attitude is good, God is pleased . . . very pleased.

Make God's will the focus of your life day by day.
If you seek to please Him and Him alone,
you'll find yourself satisfied with life.

Kay Arthur

A Parent's Tip!

Parental attitudes are contagious. It's up to you to live your life—and treat your family—in a way that pleases God because He's watching carefully . . . and so, for that matter, are your kids.

A Kid's Tip!

How can you please God? By having a good attitude, by obeying your parents and your teachers, and being kind to your friends.

Today's Prayer

Dear Lord, thank You for all
the blessings You have given me.
Today and every day I will do my best
to please You by thinking good thoughts
and doing good deeds.
Amen

Worship Him Every Day!

God is spirit, and those who worship him must worship in spirit and truth.

John 4:24 NCV

It's important to worship God on Sunday mornings, but you shouldn't stop there. You should keep worshipping Him all throughout the week. How can you do it? Well, you can worship God all week long with your prayers, your thoughts, and your good behavior.

So if you think that worship is something that only happens on Sundays, think again. You can worship God anywhere, anytime . . . and that's exactly what you should do.

He wants us to worship authentically because
it changes us—he changes us.

Sheila Walsh

A Parent's Tip!

Worship reminds you of the awesome power of God.
So worship Him daily, and allow Him to work through
you every day of the week (not just on Sundays).

A Kid's Tip!

When you worship God with a sincere heart, He will
guide your steps and bless your life.

Today's Prayer

Lord, let me worship You every day
of my life, and let me discover
the peace that can be mine when
I welcome You into my heart.
Amen

How Would Jesus Behave?

Keep your eyes on Jesus, who both begin and finished this race we're in. Study how he did it. Because he never lost sight of where he was headed, that exhilarating finish in and with God, he could put up with anything along the way: cross, shame, whatever. And now he's there, in the place of honor, right alongside God.

Hebrews 12:2 MSG

If you're not certain whether something is right or wrong, ask yourself a simple question: "How would Jesus behave if He were here?" The answer to that question will tell you what to do.

Jesus was perfect, but we are not. Still, we must try as hard as we can to be like Him. When we do, we will love others, just like Christ loves us.

WWJD = Walking With Jesus Daily.

Anonymous

A Parent's Tip!

Want them to know what Jesus would do? Then teach them what Jesus did!

A Kid's Tip!

When in doubt: do the thing that you think Jesus would do. And, of course, don't do something if you think that He wouldn't do it.

Today's Prayer

Dear Lord, let me use Jesus as my example for living. When I have questions about what to do or how to act, let me behave as He behaved. When I do so, I will be patient, loving, and kind, not just today, but every day.

Amen

Your Friend Forever

Then Jesus said, "I am the bread that gives life. Whoever comes to me will never be hungry, and whoever believes in me will never be thirsty."

John 6:35 NCV

There's an old song that says, "What a friend we have in Jesus." Those words are certainly true! When you invite Him into your heart, Jesus will be your friend forever, If you make mistakes, He'll still be your friend. If you behave badly, He'll still love you. If you feel sorry or sad, He can help you feel better if you ask Him to.

Jesus wants you to have a happy, healthy life. He wants you to behave yourself, and He wants you to take care of yourself. And now, it's up to you to do your best to live up to the hopes and dreams of your very best friend: Jesus.

Tell me the story of Jesus.
Write on my heart every word.
Tell me the story most precious,
sweetest that ever was heard.

Fanny Crosby

A Parent's Tip!

Jesus is the light of the world. As a caring parent, it's up to you to make certain that He's the light of your family, too.

A Kid's Tip!

Jesus loves me, this I know . . . but how much? Here's how much: Jesus loves you so much that He gave His life so that you might live forever with Him in heaven. And how can you repay Christ's love? By accepting Him into your heart and by obeying His rules.

Today's Prayer

Dear Lord, I am only here on this earth for a while. But, because of Your Son Jesus, I will be with You forever in heaven. Let me share that Good News with my family and friends.

Amen